Carolan's Dream

Music of the harper Turlough O'Carolan arranged for the guitar by

Keith Hinchliffe

Carolan's Dream

First produced and published in England 1996 by Dave Mallinson Publications
3 East View, Moorside, Cleckheaton, West Yorkshire, England BD19 6LD
Telephone: 01274 876388, facsimile: 01274 865208, e-mail: mally@jorum.demon.co.uk

ISBN 1 899512 37 3

A catalogue in print record for this title is available from the British Library

☐

Devised by Keith Hinchliffe
Data input and manipulation, page layout and typesetting by David J Taylor
Cover photograph of Poulnabroune Dolmen, Burren, County Clare by Liam Blake and supplied by Images Colour Library, telephone 0113 243 3389
Cover design by Bryan Ledgard, telephone 01226 766608
Printed in England by RAP Ltd, Rochdale, telephone 01706 44981
Illustrations on pages 26, 31 & 41 from Ed Sibbett Jr's *Celtic design colouring book*, published Constable and Company Ltd, ISBN 0 486 23796 6

☐

Text set in *Cochin* and display titling in *Kells*; tablature engraved using *Finale*; pages laid out in *QuarkXPress*
All tunes traditional, arrangements © Keith Hinchliffe 1993

☐

Carolan's Dream

Contents
Turlough O'Carolan 4
A note on the arrangements and tunings 4
Guide to the tablature 5
The tunes 8

Index to Tunes
Blind Mary 10
Captain O'Kane 36
Carolan's Dream 32
Carolan's Farewell to Music 42
Carolan's Quarrel with the Landlady 38
Carolan's Welcome 8
Charles O'Conor 40
Cremonea 26
Denis O'Conor, second air 28
Doctor John Stafford, or Carolan's Receipt 12
George Brabazon, second air 30
Hewlett 20
Lady Dillon 22
The Lamentation of Owen Roe O'Neill 16
Lord Inchiquin 34
Planxty Browne 27
Planxty Kelly 25
Sheebeg & Sheemore 18
Thomas Leixlip the Proud 14

All **19** transcriptions contained herein can be heard, played by Keith Hinchliffe, on the album *Carolan's Dream,* (KHCD001 and KHMC001) which is available in compact disc or cassette format from wherever you purchased this book or direct from the publishers at the address opposite

Turlough O'Carolan

THE harper and songwriter Turlough O'Carolan (1670-1738) lived through a period of painful change in Irish history. His music reflects the invasion of the old Gaelic world by the new Anglo-Irish culture that followed in the wake of Cromwell's wars. Drawing on the ancient harp tradition, native folk song and dance forms and the Italian Baroque art music which was popular amongst his wealthier patrons, Carolan's style was too eclectic and 'modern' for the more serious Celtic harpers of the time. He was, in fact, a mediocre player, having come late to the profession after losing his sight as a youth and although he made his name as a singer-songwriter, he wasn't a particularly good lyricist either. What made him so popular - and assured his immortality - was his remarkable gift for melodic invention.

Most of the tunes are named after friends or patrons of the composer and a *planxty* is such a dedicatory piece. The sub-title of **Doctor John Stafford** refers to the 'receipt' or prescription in which Stafford reversed another doctor's opinion, allowing the dejected Carolan to return to his beloved whiskey. **Sheebeg & Sheemore,** Carolan's first composition, celebrated a legendary battle between the inhabitants of two 'fairy hills'. The **Farewell to Music** was reputedly composed at the house of Mrs McDermott Roe, Carolan's first patron, shortly before his death.

Arrangements & Tunings

CAROLAN'S music has survived only through aural transmission, or as simple written melody lines; we know next to nothing about the bass parts, harmonies and decorations that the composer and his contemporaries might have used. Opinions and practice amongst modern harpers suggest that relatively simple arrangements are the most effective as well as the most 'authentic'. It is important that Carolan was playing in the days before the wire-strung, bell-toned ancient harp was superseded by the lighter sound of the gut-strung instrument. In the slower tunes particularly, there is a tendency for sustained, overlapping melody notes to form unusual, often very haunting, harmonic overtones. This effect is much more striking on the metal than on the soft-strung harp, recalling the comments of Celtic harpers about the "ringing of the harp-space" and the "harmony of freely resonating strings."

I have tried to capture some of that feeling in these arrangements for the acoustic guitar, mainly through the use of different tunings and the voicings they make possible. To take an example from the very beginning of the collection, each melody note in the first phrase of **Carolan's Welcome** has a separate string (as it would on the harp) so that a left-hand shape can be held and a suspended chord is suggested. This seems to suit the character of the tune, as it does the other minor-key melodies arranged in the same tuning. The other tunings have different harmonic characters and effects: the G major tuning, for example, offers most scope for the alternating of fretted and open strings to produce the harp-like 'ringing' or echoing effect. The left-hand fingering indications (smaller numbers) show several opportunities for amplifying these features and the guitarist will find many more.

Each tuning has its characteristic fingering patterns and, because these often require considerable stretching, I tend to use a capo, usually at the second fret. Most light-gauge strings are suitable for the G and C tunings, although a heavier bass is preferable for the low C. For GAC tunings, I recommend a heavier treble stringing for maximum effect.

All of these arrangements are played on my album **Carolan's Dream** (KHCD001 and KHMC001) which is obtainable through the publishers.

GUIDE TO THE TABLATURE

1 GENERAL

Unlike staff notation, tablature ('tab') is a *diagram* of the guitar strings. The six horizontal lines represent the strings, with the first (treble) at the top. The numbers on these lines show the frets to be fingered with the left hand (0 = an unfretted string).

Each of these numbers is close to a short vertical line or *stem* which shows the time value of the note (explained below) and makes clear which notes are to be played simultaneously. *Up* stems indicate notes to be played with right-hand *fingers* and *down* stems the notes played with the *thumb*. Smaller numbers outside the tab lines are occasionally used to recommend left-hand fingerings. (1 = index, 2 = middle etc.). These smaller numbers are often connected by short dashes (e.g. 4- … -4) to show that the finger can be kept in contact with the string to make the move to the next position easier. This does not mean that *sounding* the slide between the two notes is necessarily a good idea.

The tuning indication at the beginning of each piece begins with the bass string.

Example 1: The first bar of *Twinkle, Twinkle Little Star*

Standard tuning

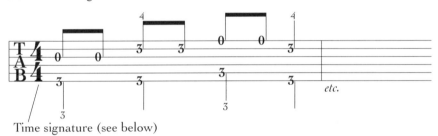

Time signature (see below)

2 TIME VALUES

The *time signature* consists of the extra-large numbers at the beginning of a piece. The *type* of time unit or beat is indicated by the lower number; the upper number indicates the *number* of such beats in a bar or measure.

If the lower number is 4, the basic unit is the *crotchet* or quarter note. The crotchet is represented by a single stem. If the lower number is 8, the unit is the *quaver* or eighth note, represented by a tailed stem (♪) except when joined together in groups (⊓, ⊓⊓ etc.). A double-tailed stem indicates a semiquaver (♬, ⊟⊟ etc.).

Example 2: *Twinkle, Twinkle* again

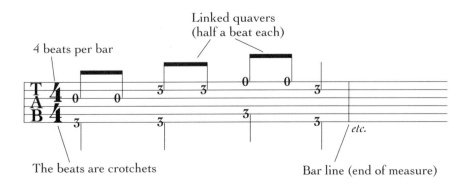

4 beats per bar

Linked quavers (half a beat each)

The beats are crotchets

Bar line (end of measure)

3 Ties

When a note lasts for more than one beat, its stem is linked by a curved line known as a *tie* to one or more 'dummy' stems with no new note-number attached, as shown in **Example 3**.

Example 3: *Greensleeves*

Standard tuning

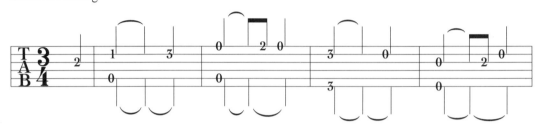

4 Dots

With time signatures based on the *quaver* (usually $\frac{6}{8}$) it's often handier to use the *dot* (as in standard notation) to show that a note's duration is increased by a *half*.

Example 4: *Greensleeves* in $\frac{6}{8}$ time

Standard tuning

5 Rests

Notes are occasionally replaced by rests, or silences, as follows:

𝄽 = crotchet rest   𝄾 = quaver rest   𝄿 = semiquaver rest.

6 Hammers, pulls, slides and other effects

Left-hand hammer-on or pull-off. The right hand plucks the first note only; further notes linked to it by the *slur,* or curved line, are sounded by the left.

Left-hand slide between the two notes. In the first example, both notes are plucked by the right hand. In the second, the right hand plays the first note only and left-hand finger pressure sounds the slide into the second note.

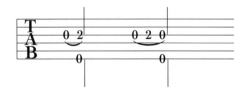

The grace note. The *grace note,* or ornament, has no stem (and no proper time value) and is played as a rapid hammer-on or pull-off (or both, as in the second example) into the main note. Grace notes should be played *on the beat,* coinciding with the bass note.

7 TRIPLETS

In crotchet-based music we often find the **triplet,** which is three evenly-spaced notes in the time of two and for which the notation is 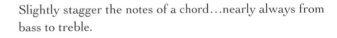 .

Example 5: *Amazing Grace*
Standard tuning

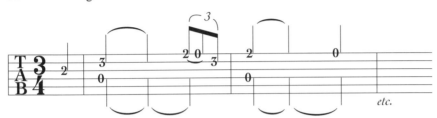

etc.

8 OTHER SIGNS

     Slightly stagger the notes of a chord…nearly always from bass to treble.

     Sustain the arrowed fretted note or chord during succeeding notes for melodic fullness or harmonic effect.

II, III etc   Roman numerals indicate a left-hand barré (one finger fretting several strings) at the numbered fret. $\frac{1}{2}$V or $\frac{1}{3}$II (for example) indicate partial barrés. A horizontal line shows the duration of the barré.

⌒   Dwell on the note or chord.

Ⓗ   A harmonic note to be played at the fret indicated.

D.C. or D.𝄋   Repeat from the beginning or from the sign 𝄋.

‖   Repeat from the beginning.

‖:   :‖   Repeat the passage enclosed by the dotted double bar lines.

1.   :‖ *2.*   After ending number 1, repeat the section (go back to the beginning or to the most recent set of dotted double bar lines) but this time finish with ending number 2 instead.

rall.   Rallentando (gradually slowing).

rit.   Ritenuto (held back in pace).

a tempo   Returning to the original pace.

Carolan's Welcome

Lively, but not fast

Tuning: CGDGAC

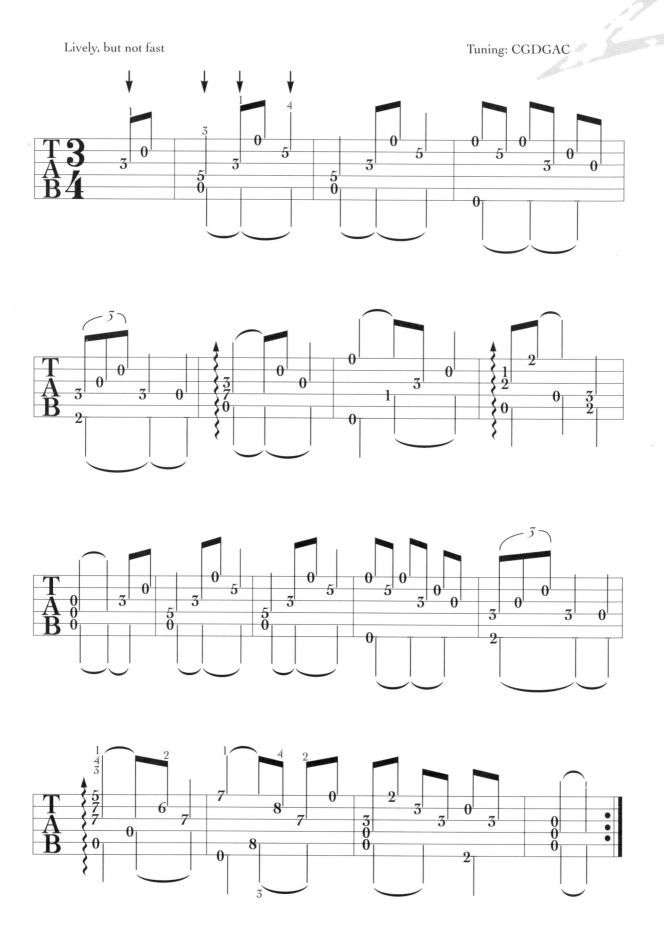

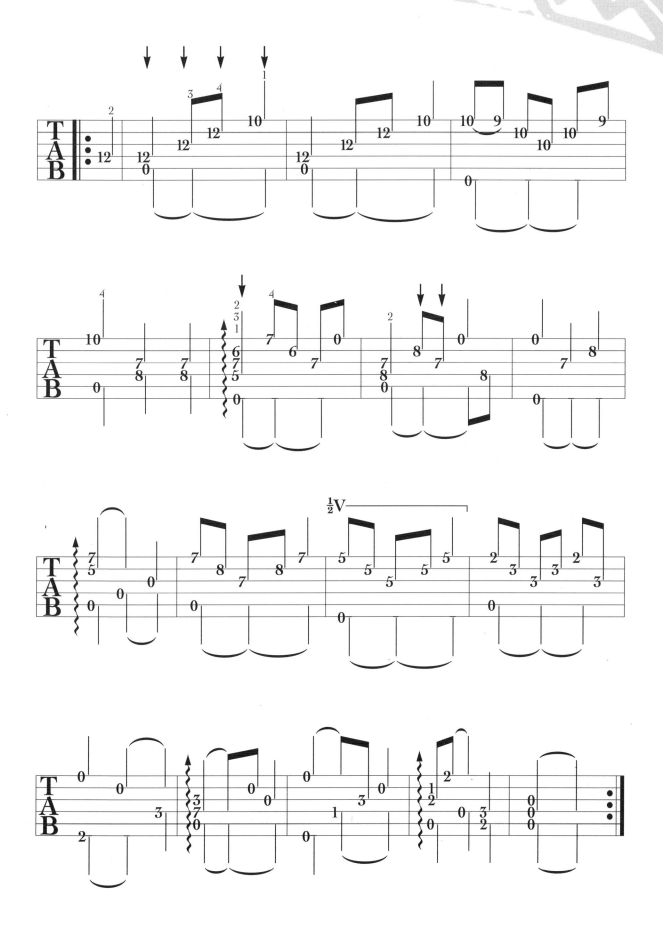

Blind Mary

Slow and emotional

Tuning: DGDGBD

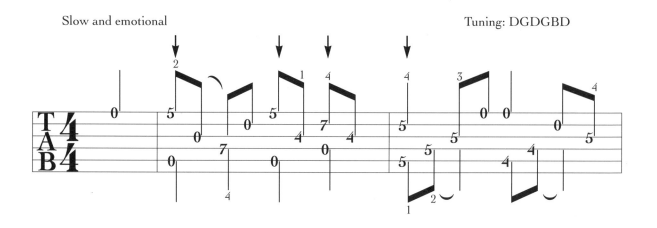

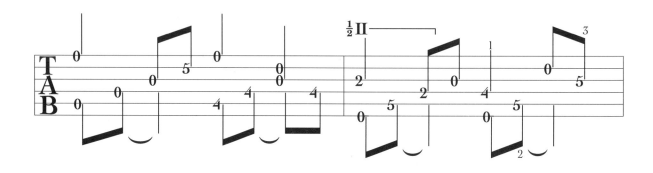

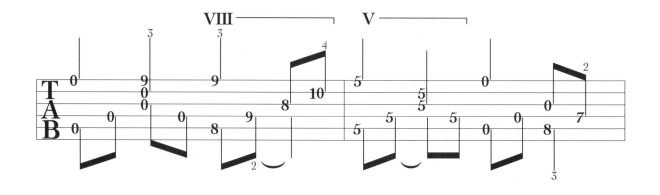

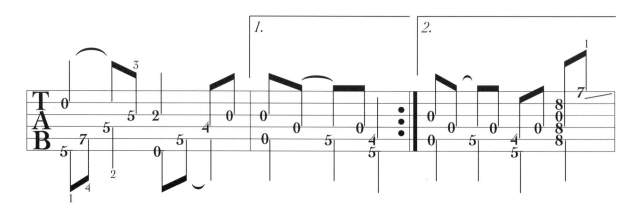

Doctor John Stafford
OR
Carolan's Receipt

Freely   Tuning: CGDGBD

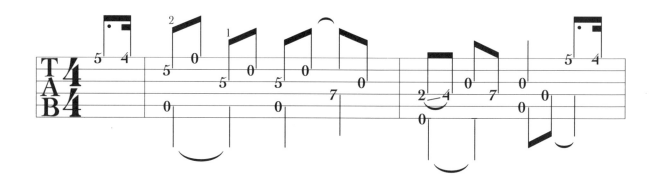

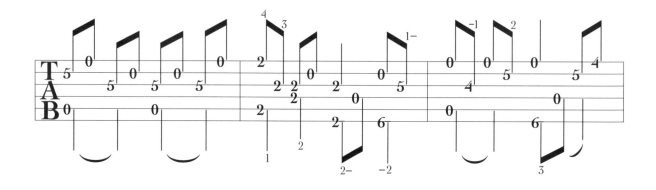

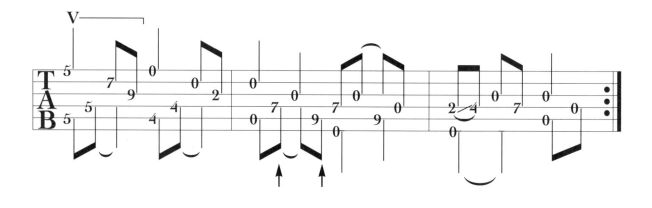

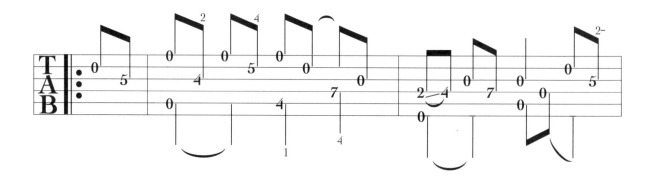

Thomas Leixlip the Proud

Fast and spirited

Tuning: CGCGCD

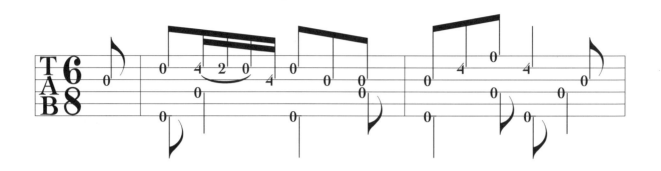

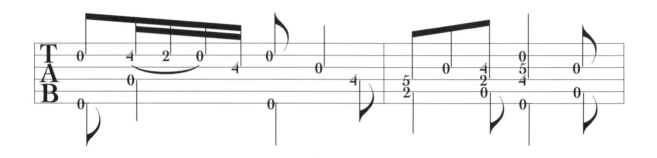

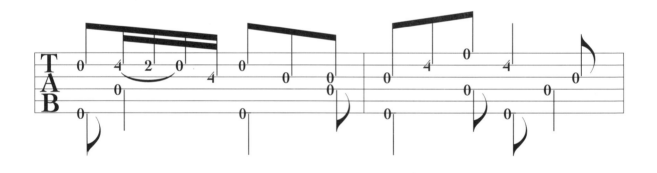

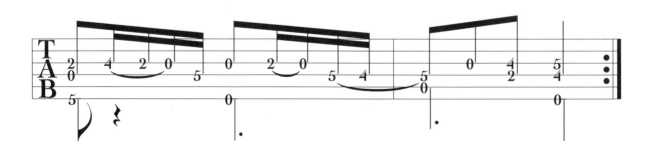

The Lamentation of Owen Roe O'Neill

Slow and dark   Tuning: CGCGCD

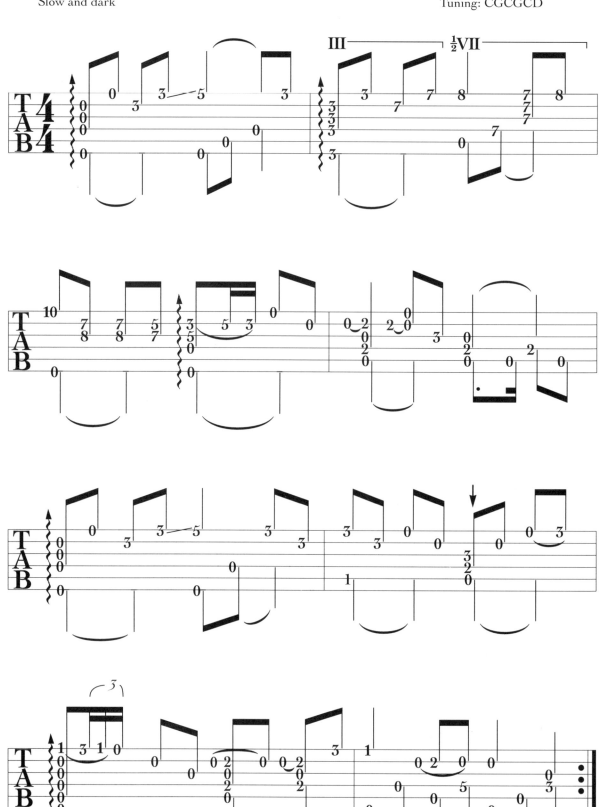

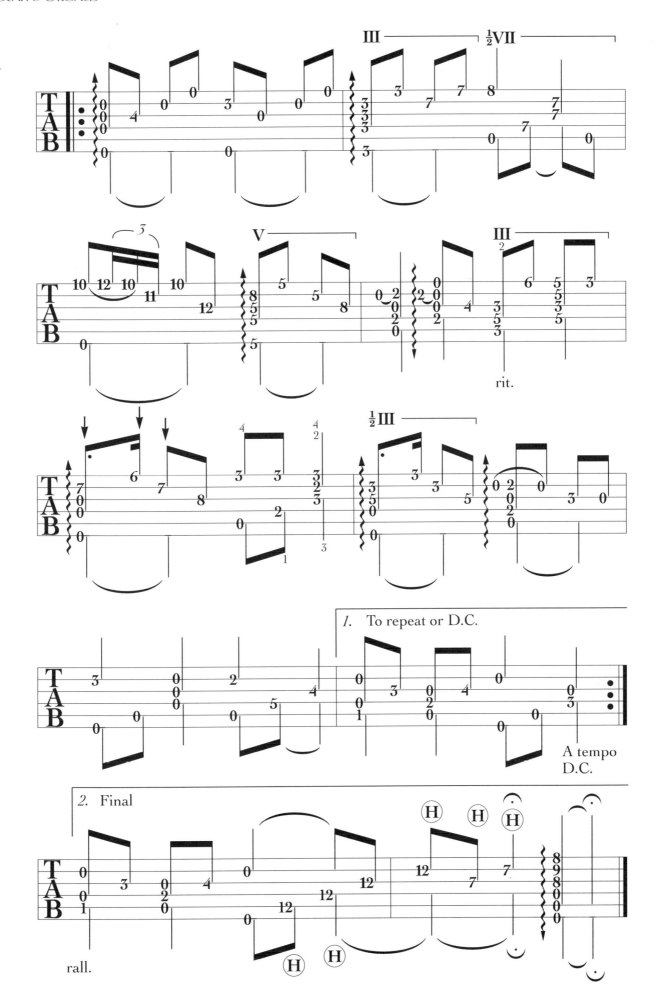

Sheebeg & Sheemore

Slowly, thoughtfully

Tuning: CGCGCD

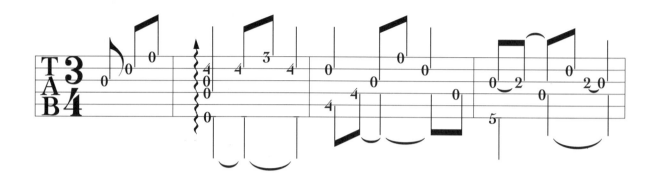

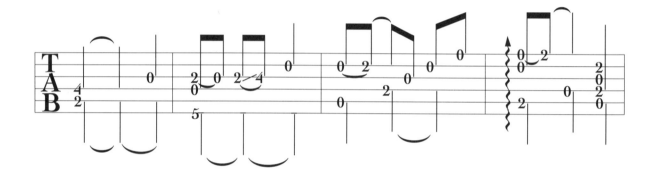

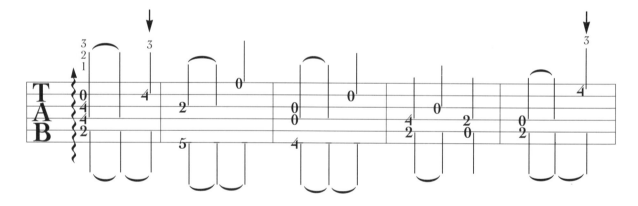

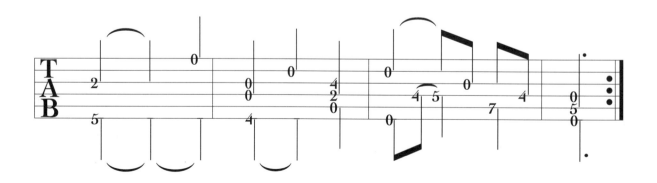

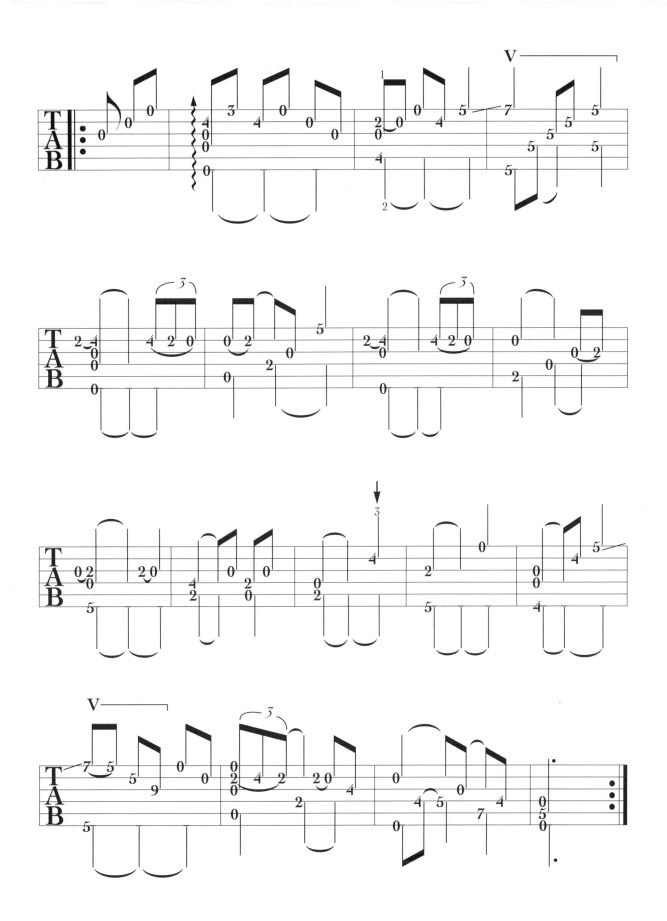

Hewlett

Lively

Tuning: CGDGBD

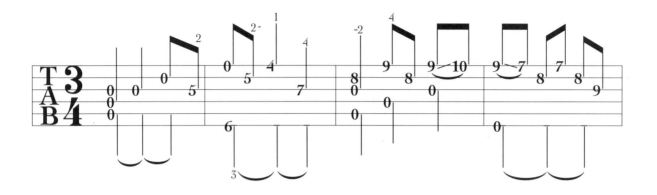

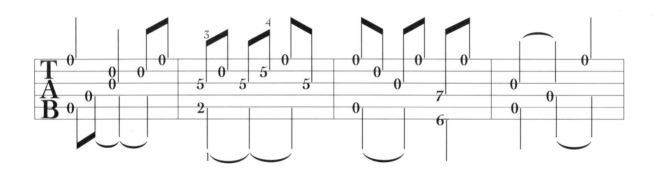

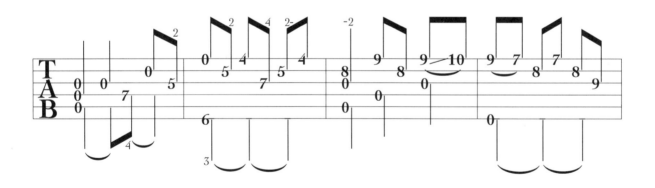

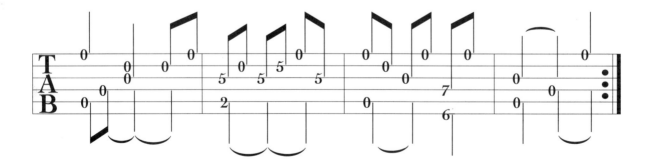

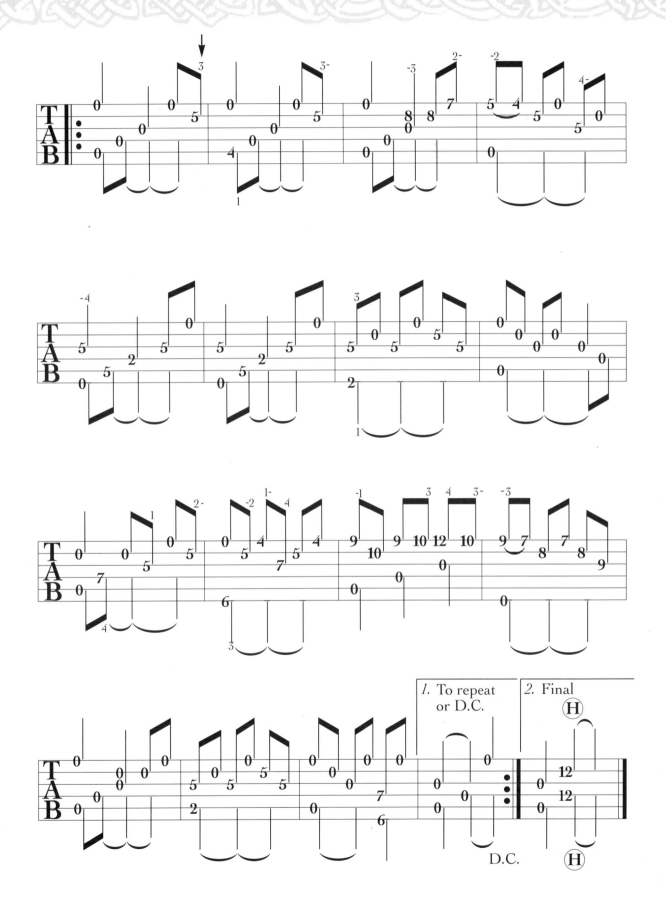

Lady Dillon

Moderately fast

Tuning: CGCGCD

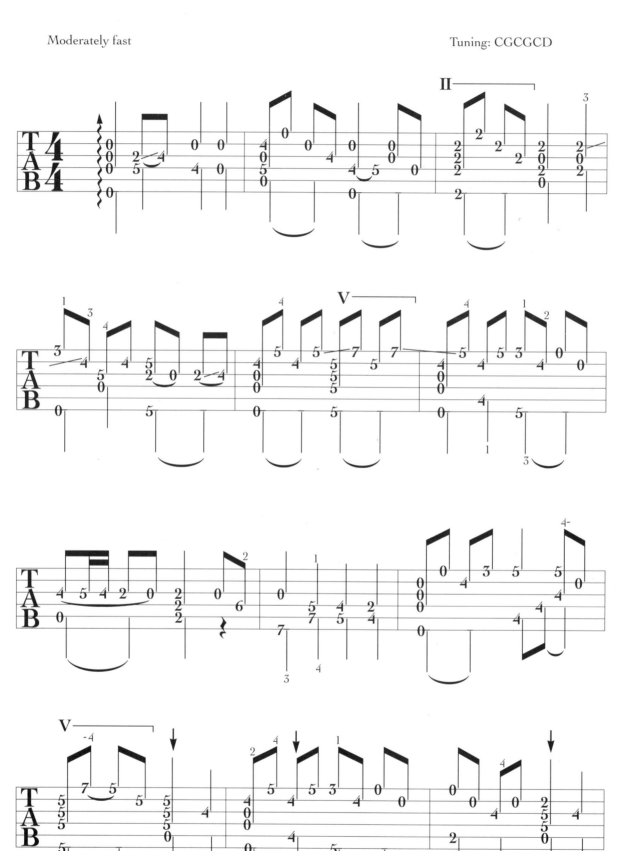

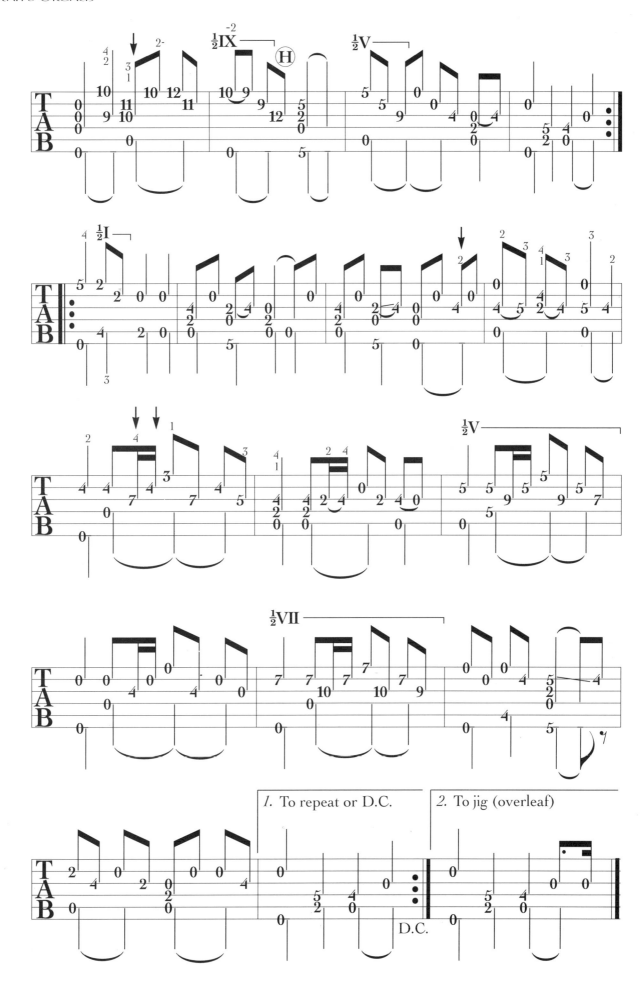

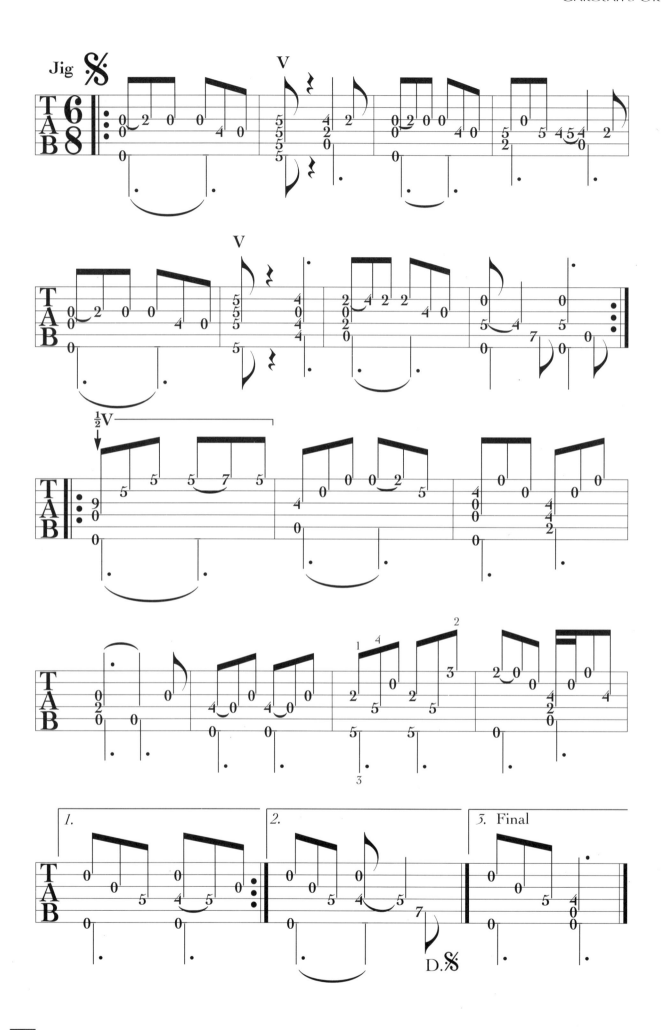

Planxty Kelly

Almost a slow march

Tuning: CGCGCD

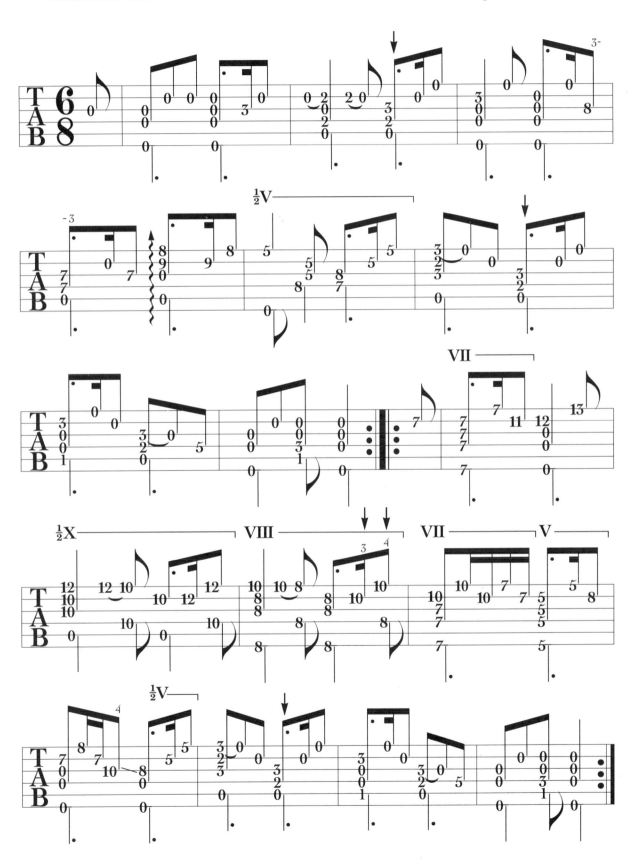

25

CREMONEA

Moderately

Tuning: DGDGAC

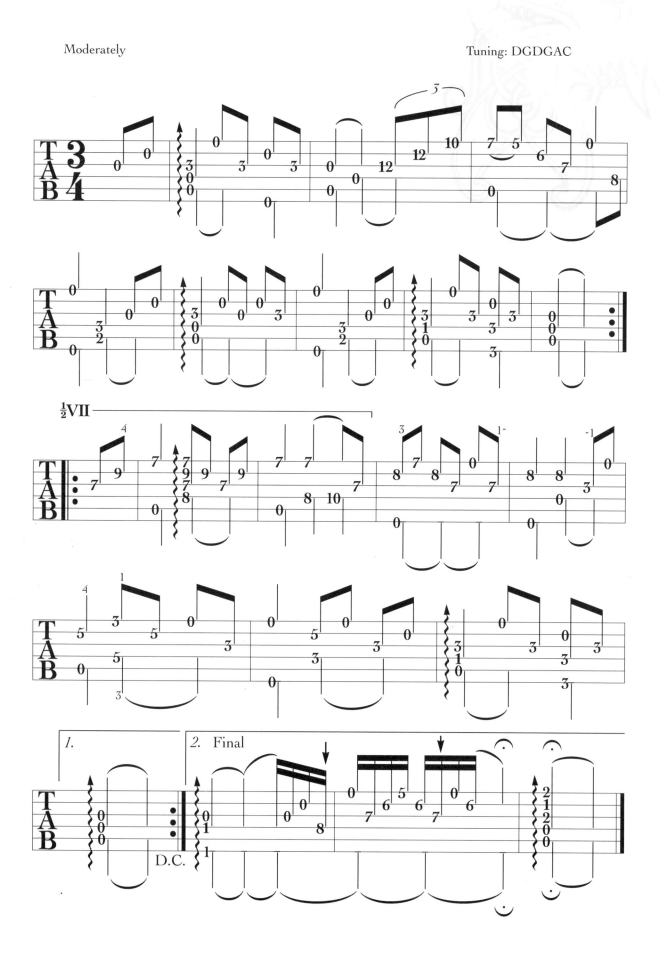

Planxty Browne

With a bounce

Tuning: DGDGBD

Denis O'Conor, second air

Very lively

Tuning: DGDGAC

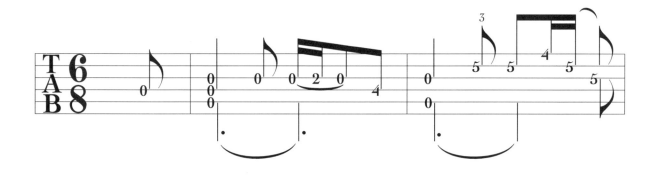

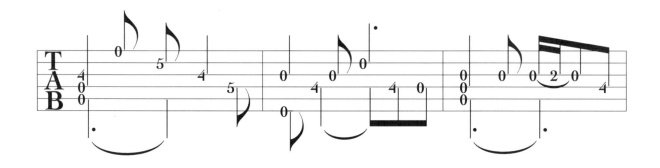

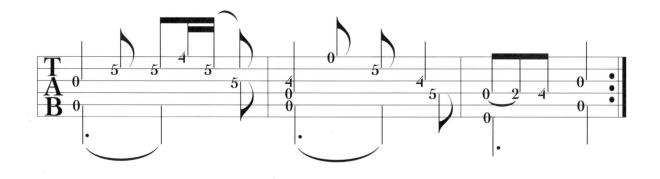

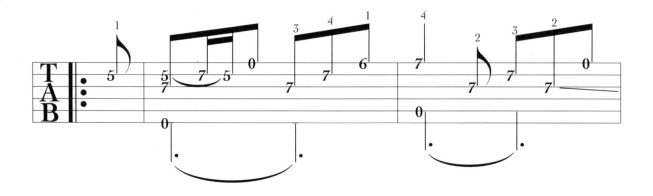

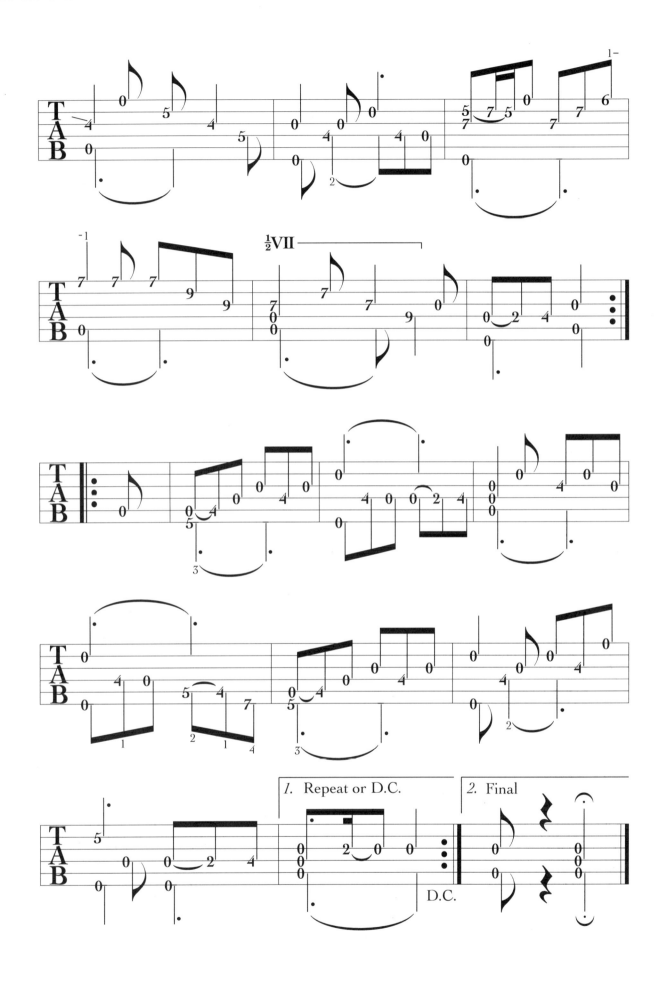

George Brabazon, second air

Fast but flowing

Tuning: DGDGBD

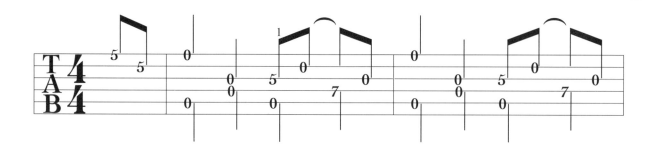

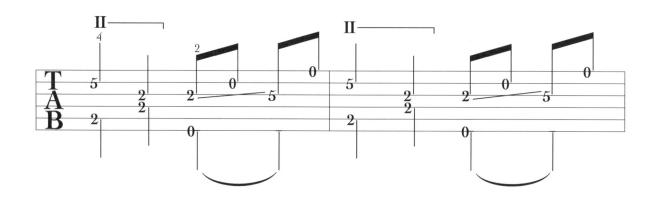

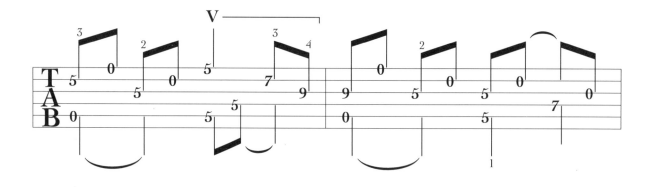

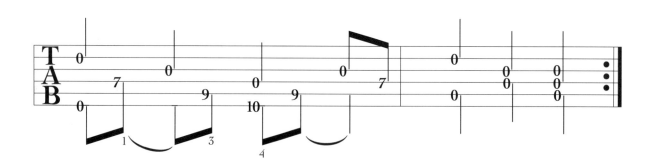

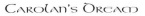

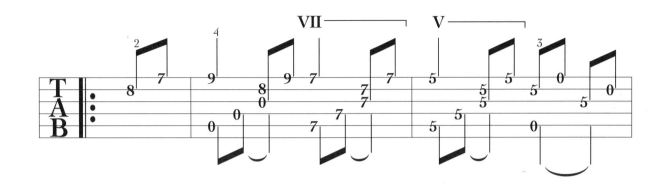

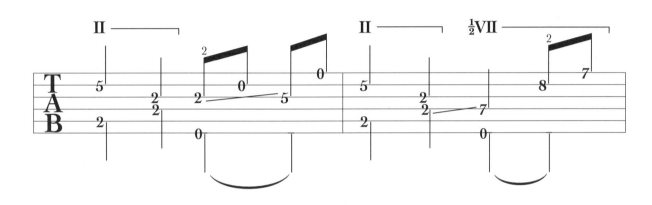

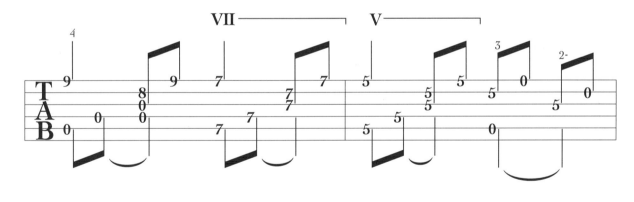

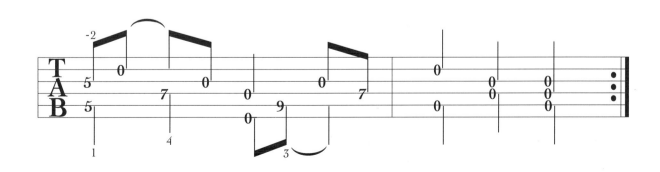

Carolan's Dream

Slowly and expressively

Tuning: CGDGAC

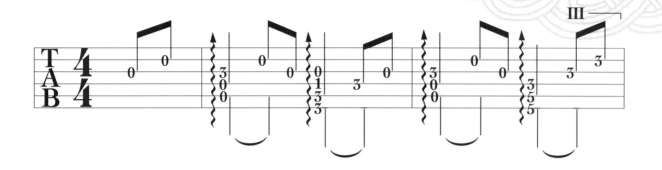

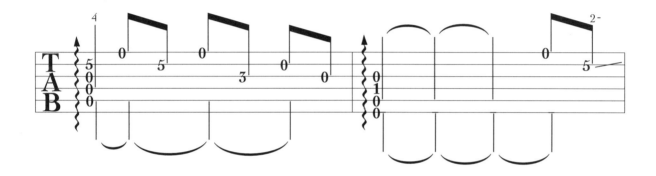

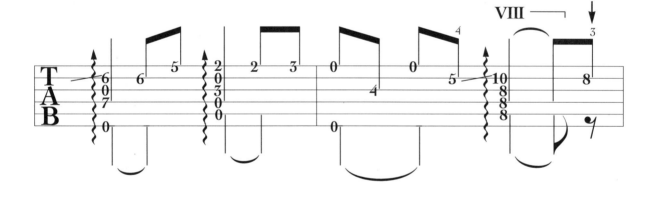

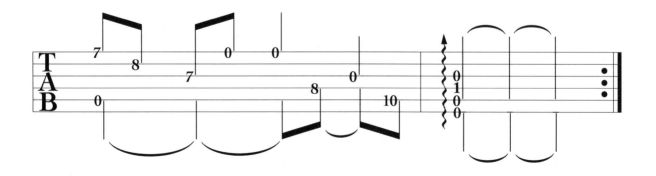

Copyright 1996 © Keith Hinchliffe & Dave Mallinson Publications

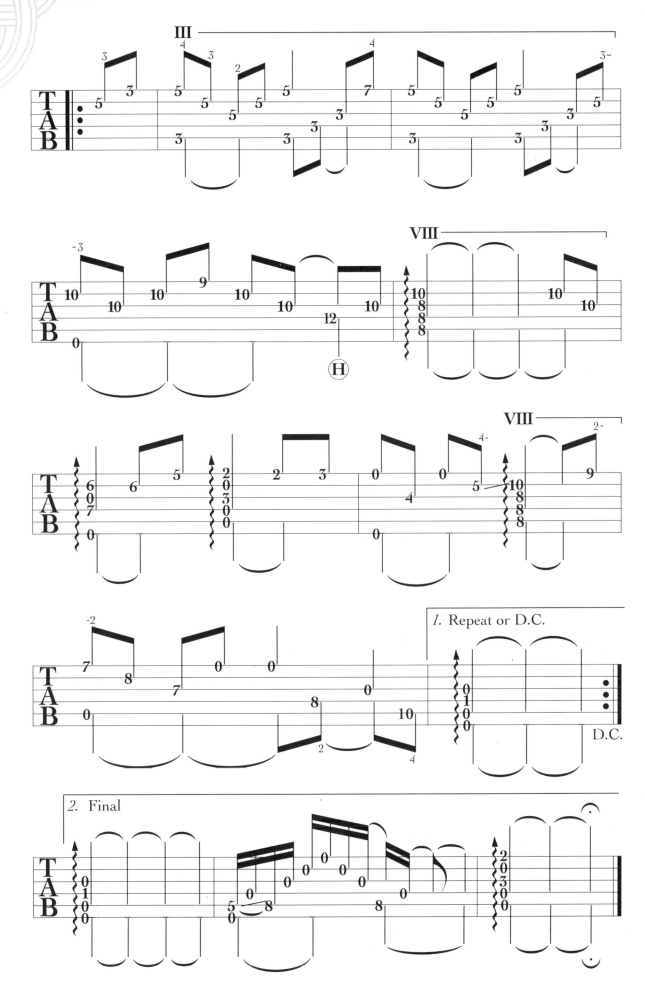

Lord Inchiquin

Lively, but not too fast

Tuning: CGCGCD

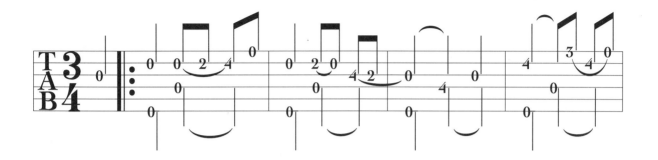

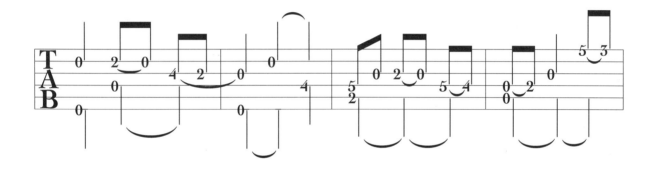

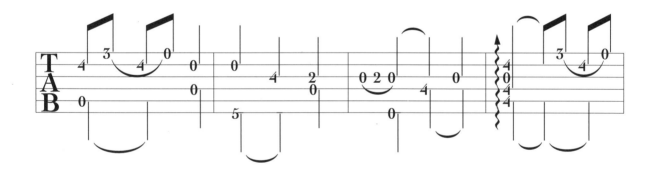

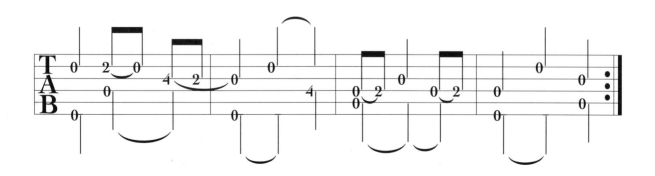

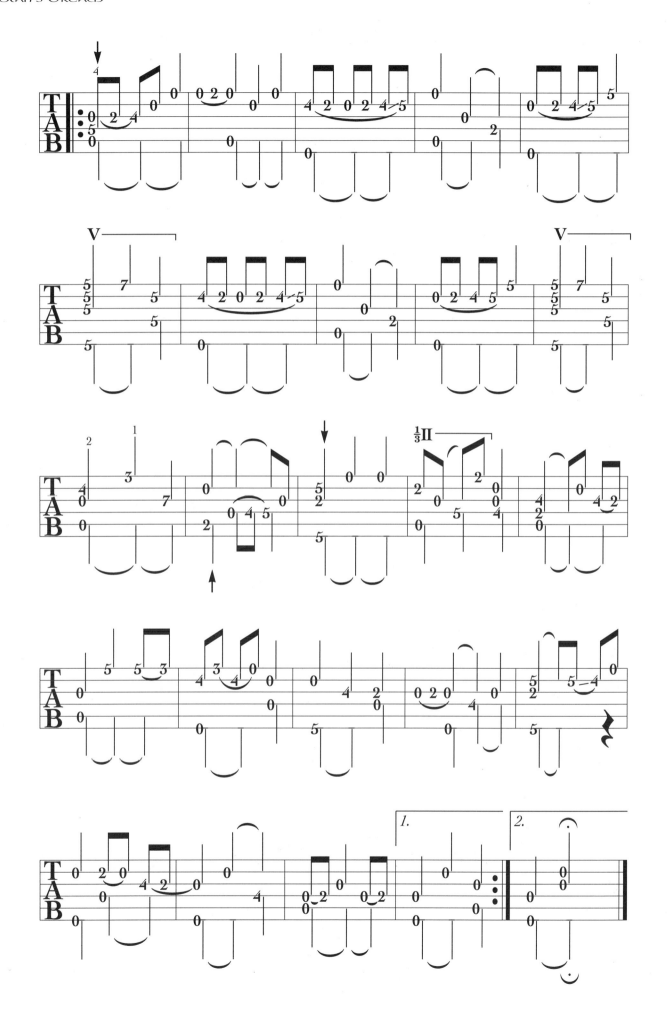

Captain O'Kane

Held back   Tuning: DGDGAC

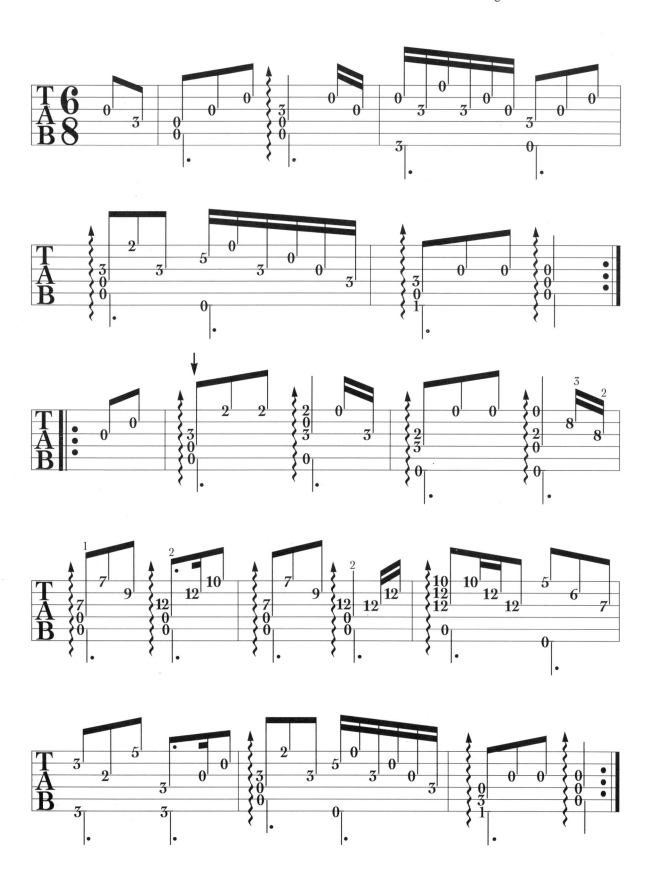

Variation

Carolan's Quarrel with the Landlady

Wistfully

Tuning: CGDGBD

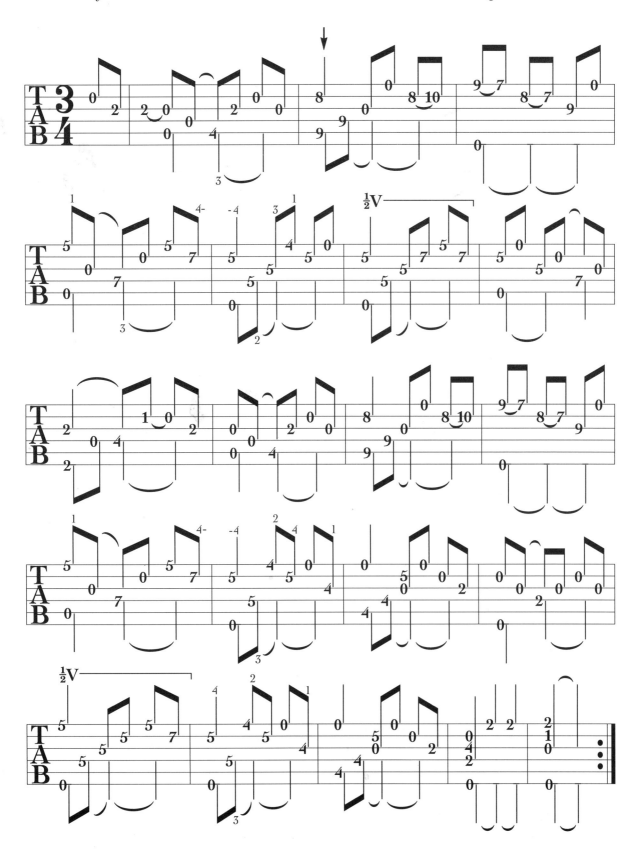

Charles O'Conor

Spiritedly

Tuning: CGCGCE

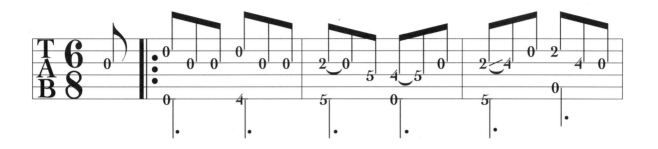

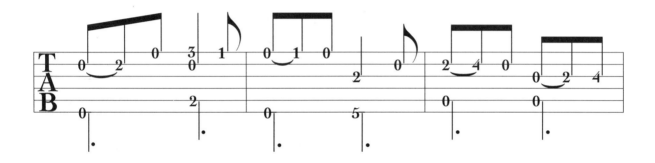

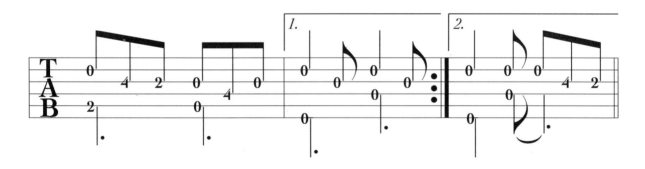

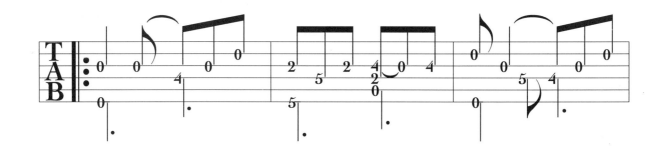

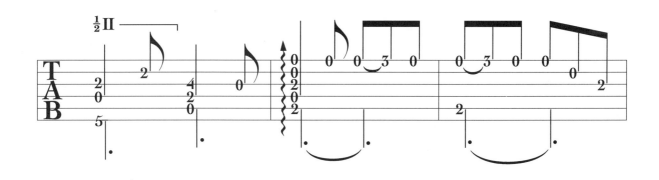

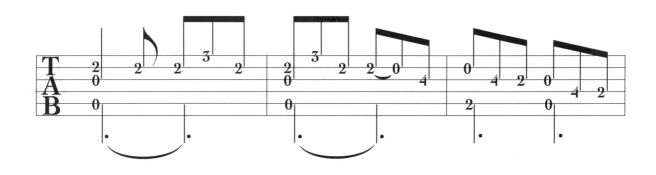

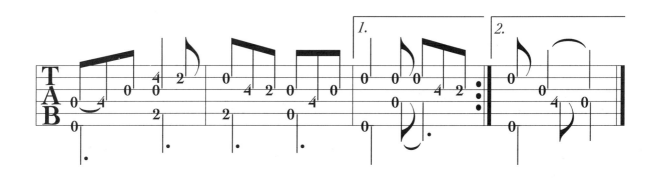

Carolan's Farewell to Music

Very slowly and majestically

Tuning: CGCGCD

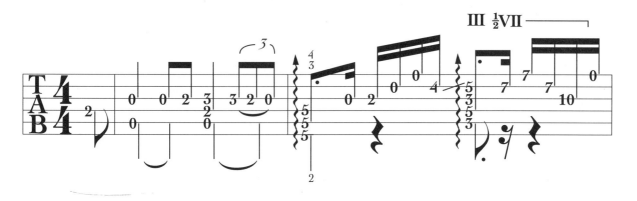

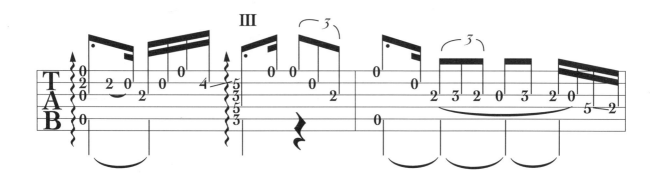

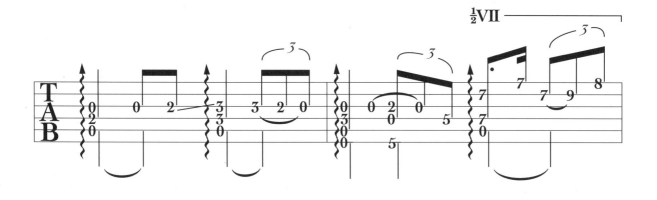

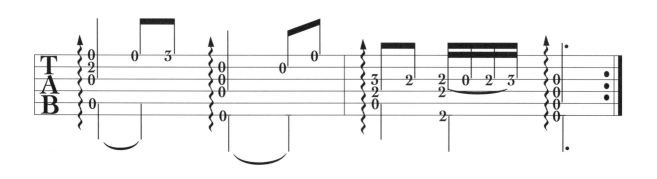

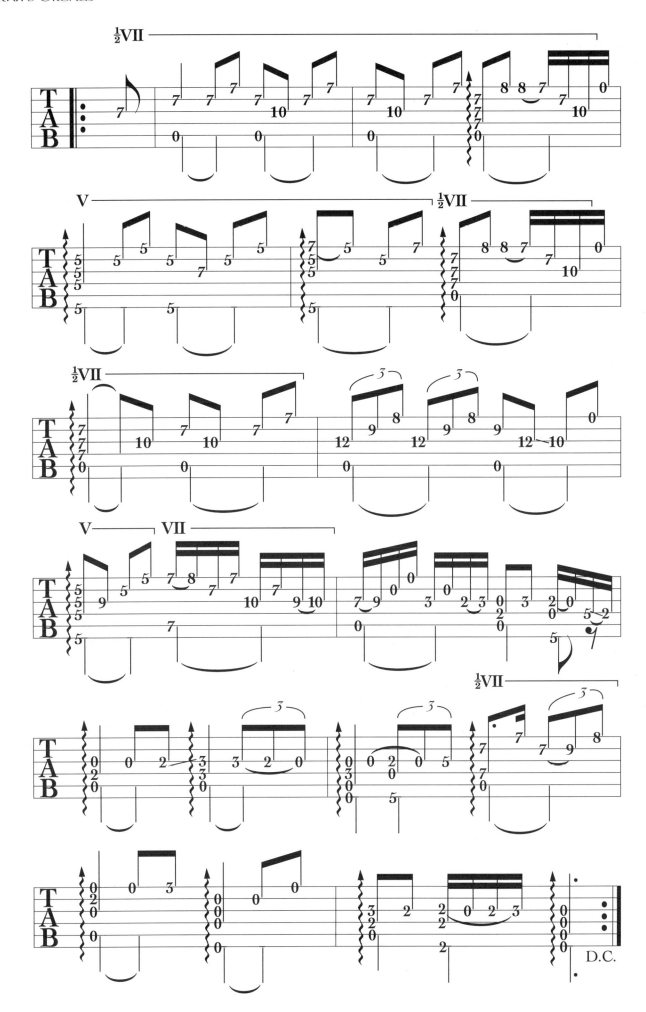

Final variation on second part